The Clever Tykes Books

Write-it Ryan

Illustrated by Sam Moore

To standing out, not blending in

Chapter 1: Pens down, please!

Captain Steg, the dinosaur superhero, flew high up into the sky. The nearby golden mountains were covered in storm clouds but the weather report said it would be sunny everywhere. Something was wrong!

Captain Steg charged through the sky and gave a deafening "ROOAAARRR!" With all his might he blew the storm clouds away and revealed the hidden zombie wizard fortress.

The wizards had been discovered! They floated out of the castle and into the sky; their faces cold and lifeless as they called out for brains to eat.

"Brains! Yummy brains" they wailed but...

"Put your pens down!" barked Miss Butters. Class 7B dropped their pens, trembling in fear. No one disobeyed Miss Butters!

In today's English lesson, 7B were set the difficult task of writing an exciting cliffhanger and **someone** hadn't finished...

Captain Steg shook his head. "No brains for you, you evil zombie wizards!" He charged towards them...

Ryan paused. What would happen next? Maybe the zombie wizards should win. That'd shock the pants off some people!

Writing stories was Ryan's favourite thing to do. Ever. He created amazing new worlds where incredible things happened. He wrote stories about evil wizards, superhero dinosaurs, giant dogs and princesses who only ate paper! He often forgot where he was when his imagination took over.

"I said put your pens down, NOW!" roared

Miss Butters. Even the tables and chairs shuddered in terror.

To Ryan's annoyance, San was nudging him. "Stop that, San! I have to finish writing this battle!" insisted Ryan.

San nudged him even harder, "Ryan!" he whispered loudly. "Put your pen down. Quick!"

It was too late. Miss Butters' shadow crept over Ryan's desk, as she loomed in front of him like a creepy gargoyle.

Ryan gulped.

"Erm. But. Well. I. Story. Sorry." He stopped trying to apologise. He didn't want to make the gargoyle even angrier.

Miss Butters stood staring at Ryan silently. She didn't move. She didn't blink. She just stared.

Everyone was silent. *No one* disobeyed Miss Butters!

Ryan felt his heartbeat drumming in his ears.

Th-thump. Th-thump. Th-thump.

Miss Butters picked up his story and slithered away. She slinked through the desks collecting everyone's work.

Ryan looked at San, who shrugged his shoulders. How much trouble was he in?

Miss Butters returned to the front of the class. "I will now read out some of the work you have done. I can already see some of you will be staying in during lunchtime."

Everyone looked at each other. Who would be Miss Butters' first victim?

"Ah, yes. Tim. Your work was interesting. Nice try but you will have to write more than just your name during lunchtime. Stay behind." Tim sank down in his chair, wishing he hadn't spent the whole lesson doodling on the desk.

"Sally. You wrote a lot but I didn't ask you to describe what you watched on television last night. You will stay behind and TRY AGAIN."

Sally opened her mouth in shock, wide enough to fit a possum inside. She was going to miss out on all the lunchtime gossip with Jamie-May and Chardonnay.

One by one, evil Miss Butters gave detentions to the students of 7B.

"Now let's read Ryan's story. It must have been very important to continue writing after I told everyone to stop!" Ryan sat petrified as Miss Butters read his story aloud...

Chapter 2: The school report

The class listened intently as Miss Butters read Ryan's story about Captain Steg and the zombie wizards, right to the very end.

"...this was it. The final battle! Who will win???"

There was a short moment of silence...

...then the classroom erupted with cheers and applause!

"Mate, that was awesome!" said San, patting Ryan on the back.

“A-ma-zing!” added Sally. “I am totally going to tell *all* my friends about that battle.”

“QUIET!” shrieked Miss Butters. “I have NOT finished speaking!”

Terrified, class 7B fell silent once more.

"Very good, Ryan," said Miss Butters, “you have a wonderful imagination and writing skills.” Ryan sat in shock. Sally gasped. Tim rocked so far back he fell off his chair. Ryan was sure he was in for a year’s worth of detention!

The lunchtime bell rang loudly. Everyone grabbed their schoolbags and charged towards the door.

“Wait one moment!” howled Miss Butters. “Some of you are NOT LEAVING!” She clung on to the doorframe to stop anyone getting past. “And

EVERYONE will be taking their school reports home today!"

7B groaned as a smirk flickered across Miss Butters' face. "Some of your parents will not be very happy with your grades for English." She glared at Sally and Tim who shamefully lowered their heads.

"There are, however, some of you who have done rather well," she continued, her eyes now fixed on Ryan, "Your parents might like what they read."

***

As soon as Ryan arrived home, he nervously handed his school report to Dad, who began reading.

“Hmm. Yes. Ah-hum. Yes. Hmm.”

The smartest computer in the world wouldn't be able to work out what Dad was thinking. His strange hums were like an alien language.

"It's not bad," Dad sighed eventually. "According to Miss Butters you are doing well in English."

Miss Butters never seemed to like anything. Perhaps magic elves had stolen the real school reports and sent out silly ones instead.

"What do you want to be when you grow up?" asked Dad, bringing Ryan back to earth.

"I want to be an author," admitted Ryan. He wanted to write books for children about wonderful tales filled with adventure and magic.

Dad sighed again. "There are not many jobs for authors, or any kind of writers, Ryan. It's a very competitive world. People must like the stories you create. How many people have read your stories?"

"Well, just me," admitted Ryan, "but..." Dad interrupted before Ryan could tell him about everyone cheering his story in class.

"I want you to focus on your other subjects. It looks like you could do much better in science and maths," said Dad assertively.

He stood up and ruffled Ryan's hair. "It's okay kiddo. I'm sure you will grow to like maths and science, you might find a job using those."

Ryan didn't want to stop writing stories. Whenever he was feeling sad, his writing would take him to another universe, forgetting about homework and evil teachers. Unfortunately for Ryan, Dad was more concerned with his grades and was already devising 'exciting' ways to help him.

"I'll make maths and science more exciting. You can use maths to work how much we pay for our electricity bill. Or we can read the ingredients on the washing powder box and see all the chemicals it contains!" Dad beamed.

Unconvinced, Ryan trudged up the stairs to his bedroom. One last time, he began to write.

"There, just next to our world, is another world. It's a place where things are lost but never found. Have you ever lost a sock or some keys? This is the world that they go to, this is the World of the Lost!"

Chapter 3: A secret project

The next morning, Ryan decided to pay Miss Butters a visit before school started.

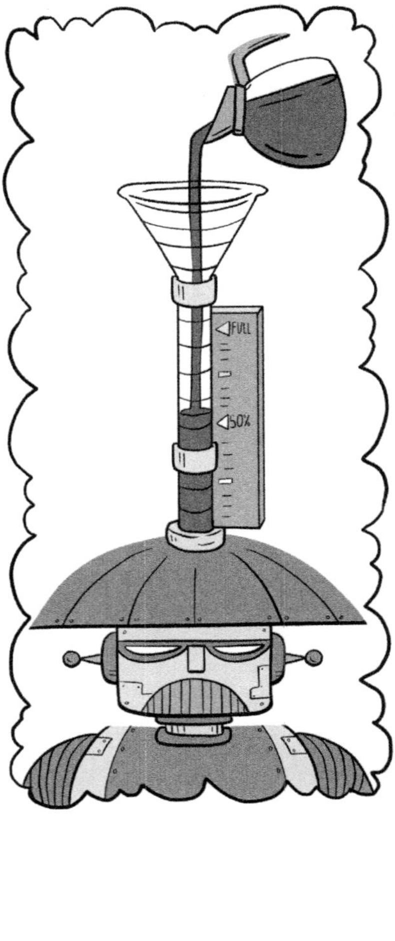

Miss Butters was slurping her coffee. In fact, lots of teachers slurped coffee. Ryan wondered if teachers were actually coffee-powered machines. How could he stop the evil drones from taking over the world?

Nervously, Ryan approached her desk, wincing as the horrid stench struck his nose.

"Oh, hello, Ryan. Are you okay?" asked Miss Butters. Ryan avoided breathing through his nose as she took another long swig of her coffee.

"My dad said I shouldn't write anymore. He told me it would be difficult to find a job as a writer," Ryan blurted out.

"Bwwhaaat?" Miss Butters spluttered her coffee all over her desk.

Mega-disaster! Ryan had interrupted Miss Butters before she was fully refuelled; she was conking out right in front of him!

"You should never give up on something you enjoy," Miss Butters recovered. "You are very good at writing, Ryan - follow your dreams."

Ryan looked uncertainly at Miss Butters. Coffee fuel dripped off the desk onto his shoes. He thought it best not to say anything.

"It won't be easy, Ryan, but nothing worthwhile is easy. I know many talented writers who love doing it.

They were just like you once!" She started dabbing up the spilt coffee on her desk.

"In fact, from now on, your English homework will be a secret project. I want you to write a story from start to finish. You can surprise your dad with it when it's complete."

Ryan's eyes lit up, He had a secret mission. "Wow! But how do I improve my grades in maths and science?" He imagined his dad finding out he had failed maths and exploding in the living room.

Miss Butters smiled. "You need to manage your time carefully. Prove to your dad you can write a great story and improve your grades at the same time!"

Miss Butters turned on her laptop and wiped coffee from the screen. “I’ll create a blog page for you. Each week you will write a chapter of your story and post it as a blog.“

Ryan had never heard this strange word before. Maybe it was some weird blobby log. It wouldn’t be easy to write on.

Miss Butters noticed Ryan’s confusion. “A blog is like a page for you to write your stories on. Except this time, it will be on the internet!”

“What? So everyone can read it?” he asked excitedly. This was the best secret mission ever.

“Exactly” confirmed Miss Butters as she finished setting up the page. “Bazillions of people earn a living through their writing, lots of them use blogs to do it. I want to see your first chapter before the end of this week!”

The morning bell rang, which was Ryan’s cue to hurry to morning registration.

“Thank you, Miss Butters!” said Ryan, darting away. “You’re not as scary as everyone says.”

Miss Butters’ hair stood on end and her eyes turned red. “Scary? Who said I was scary? I’m ALWAYS nice!" she harked angrily after Ryan, who was running for his life down the corridor.

"I AM NICE!"

Chapter 4: Plotting

"I can't start it tonight" thought Ryan, walking home after another busy day at school. Mr Adder had handed out tonnes of maths homework as usual. Ryan suspected Mr Adder was an imposter who gave homework to students to research his sinister plots!

"Dad, do we have a calendar anywhere?" called Ryan arriving home.

"Are you making sure you have time to study for maths and science? That's very smart of you Ryan," chuckled Dad proudly. Ryan nodded in agreement, avoiding any mention of stories. He was on a secret story-writing mission and there was no way Dad was finding out!

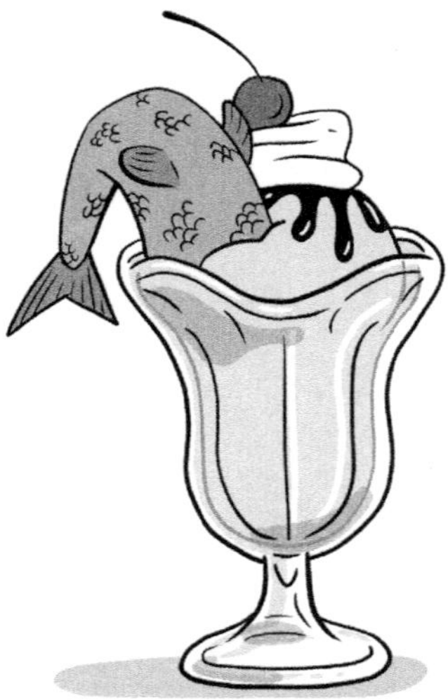

Dad stirred some beef into a bowl of cheesecake mix. Yesterday they had curried strawberries. The day before they had a fish sundae for dessert. Ryan dreaded the thought of what he would be eating tonight.

"I think we have one in the cupboard. It's buried under a lot of stuff, though. I'll need your help," said Dad, taking off his apron and leaving the beef cheesecake to simmer gruesomely.

The cupboard under the stairs was a treasure trove of bizarre items. There were Christmas decorations and plant pots and loose keys to unlock every door imaginable. There were old shoelaces and old batteries, inkless pens and ticket stubs for the cinema. Ryan knew Dad must need all these things for something very important.

Buried deep in the darkest corner was something Ryan could never have imagined. Dad grimaced as he slowly pulled out a mysterious tube of paper.

Ryan scrunched up his face in disgust as Dad unrolled the paper. It was horrific! There in Dad's hands was a calendar - a calendar of kittens!

"Aww, man! Dad, I can't use this!"

On every month, creepy kittens were staring back at anyone who dared to look them in the eye. Ryan looked away; it would be unwise to stare for too long or the kittens would steal your soul.

Dad shrugged his shoulders. "Sorry kiddo. It was a present from your Aunt Laurette, this will have to do."

Ryan reluctantly pinned the calendar to his wall. Kittens were riding ocean waves on surfboards. Kittens sat wide-eyed in carved pumpkins. Kittens were wearing Christmas hats. In every picture, the creepy kittens stared soullessly at Ryan.

Taking out his lucky pen, Ryan quickly drew sunglasses and moustaches on the kittens and marked the days when he could study maths and science. He marked the days when he could take time to relax.

Finally, he secretly marked when he could work on the chapters for his blog!

"Dinner is ready," Dad called from downstairs, "I can't wait for you to 'meat' dessert!" Ryan shuddered. He wasn't sure which he preferred, the creepy kittens or Dad's crazy cooking.

***

The next day, Ryan worked the hardest that anyone had ever worked at school. He tried answering questions even if he wasn't sure of the answer, he actually knew more than he thought! As soon as Ryan got home he pulled out his notepad and set to work finding ideas for his story.

"Maybe I could write about a desert filled with travelling circuses?" he said spinning his lucky pen before scribbling down notes. "All of the clowns would be in a high-speed race to reach a wish-making lamp-post!"

“Hmmm. I know! I’ll create a tale about an opera-singing polar bear seeking fame and fortune in the year 2514.”

Ryan glanced at the growing list of ideas on the paper in front of him. Hmm, none of them would make a story. What was his story?

Ryan needed help.

Chapter 5: Where to start?

"Dad?" asked Ryan. "How do you come up with the recipes for your disgu-, err, delicious meals?" Ryan knew Dad must be very creative to conjure up such bizarre combinations of food.

"I like to clear my mind," said Dad, eagerly. "The ideas come when I'm not thinking about anything else. Is this for a science project?"

Ryan nodded. "Yes of course it is *all* for science," he fibbed.

"Try staring at a blank surface, clear your mind, just like a painter stares at a blank canvas," suggested Dad, "or try meditating!"

Ryan used his time in the bath as an opportunity to clear his mind. Surrounded by warm bubbly water, he already felt relaxed. The bathroom wall wasn't exactly blank, but he stared at it anyway.

He stared.

And he stared.

And he stared a little more.

And he carried on staring.

Slowly but surely thoughts crept into his head. *Why were these tiles square and not triangle tiles? Why were tiles called 'tiles'? How many tiles were there on the wall?*

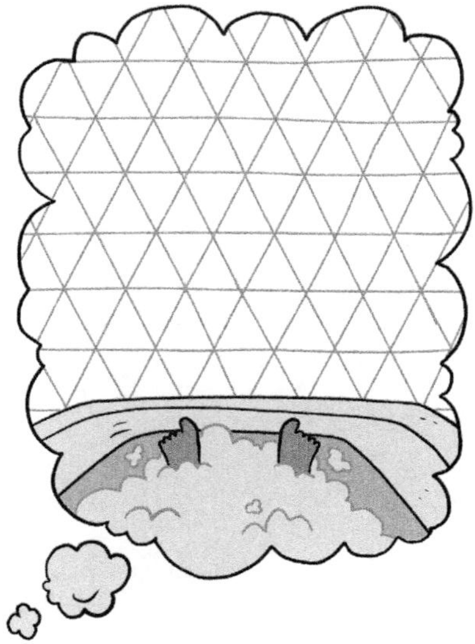

All he could think about were tiles!

Tiles would never make a good story. Ryan gave up

on having a bath, and stomped off to his room in frustration. It was time to try meditating.

"I am clearing my mind," said Ryan to himself, crossing his legs and closing his eyes. He took a deep breath, exhaled and repeated, "I am clearing my mind".

“I am freeing myself of confusion,” continued Ryan. He broke into a gentle hum to focus his mind. Ryan hummed for a few minutes.

Ryan couldn’t believe it; he was humming without even trying. Was this peace? Was he having some strange experience where his body and mind had become one? Had Ryan mastered some magnificent form of meditation?

The humming stopped; followed by a bang and a clang! That certainly wasn’t him. He got up and pressed his ear against the wall. It was the boiler!

Ryan collapsed onto his bed and sighed. How was he going to decide on a story? No way was he going to be foiled by boring tiles or a noisy boiler.

***

The students of 7B ran for their lives as another English lesson came to an end. Sally and her friends had been giggling at the words 'nincompoop' and 'poppycock' from an old book they were reading. Miss Butters was not impressed.

Ryan bravely stayed behind to tell an annoyed-looking Miss Butters about his problem.

She took a sip of coffee, which seemed to cheer her up slightly. “Creative people are always filled with ideas, Ryan. Stop thinking about your blog and focus on your maths and science.”

“But, but...“ Ryan should have thought of a story sooner, was the secret project already over?

“The idea for your story will come when you least expect it,” interrupted Miss Butters. “Use this time to study your other subjects.”

For the rest of that week, Ryan put extra effort into studying maths and science. He thought carefully about answers and asked for help if he needed it. As hard as he tried, Ryan still felt frustrated that he had no idea for his story.

Chapter 6: Meals from Mars

"Ryan, which would cost more: two of these jars of pickled onion or three tubs of coleslaw?" Dad jumped from one aisle to the next, "How about this pasta? Do you know how we grow pasta?"

The weekly supermarket shop had turned into a tacky game show and Dad was the host. Ryan covered his face as people gave them funny looks.

"Ah, ha! Pasta doesn't grow! We have to make it."

This was the worst shopping trip ever.

"Ah, yes! Salad leaves!" Dad exclaimed excitedly, spotting the leafy greens section.

"Science question time! How many planets are in our solar systems?" asked Dad.

"Six," Ryan guessed quietly, shrugging his shoulders.

"Ooh, nice try. There are eight planets." Dad held a tomato aloft. "This one is close to our planet. It's called Mars."

“Is that where you find your dinner recipes?” joked Ryan, sarcastically; he knew Dad was only helping him understand how important maths and science were.

Dad stopped bouncing around and looked at Ryan, stunned. “But- but- I thought my meals were the tastiest dishes ever! Tonight I’m making a cheesy, chocolate chicken treat.”

This was as good a time as any for Ryan to admit his hatred of Dad’s exotic dishes, especially fish sundaes. There was no going back now.

“Dad, I’m sorry but I don't think anyone else on Earth would dare to eat the meals that you create. They’re like meals from...from...” Ryan stopped.

That was it! What if Dad's disgusting dinner ideas actually DID come from outer space?

An alien chef crash-lands on Earth. He starts making his alien meals for celebrities. A secret spy service tries to capture the alien chef for experiments! There would be an epic chase through the dusty desert as the alien flees for freedom.

That was Ryan's story!

Ryan's head was buzzing. Dad, meanwhile, looked confused at Ryan's sudden pause in the supermarket.

"Is everything okay, kiddo?" he asked.

"Oh, erm, Mars. Yes, Mars, I just remembered I have some science homework to do," said Ryan.

They quickly finished shopping and journeyed home. Ryan helped Dad unpack before darting to his bedroom. He turned on his laptop and loaded his blog page. It was time to write the first chapter of *Meals from Mars*!

"Looking forward to your cheesy, chocolate, chicken dinner?" Dad shouted up the stairs.

There was no response.

"Ryan?" he called.

Still no response.

Puzzled, Dad crept up the stairs to see what Ryan was up to. Ryan was so busy typing he couldn't hear him coming. Was Dad about to discover the secret project? Dad slowly pushed open the bedroom door and peered inside, he saw Ryan writing something about Mars and spaceships!

Dad glared at the screen. "Hehe" he chuckled quietly, "looks like science homework!"

Not to disturb Ryan, Dad crept back downstairs and started making the 'delicious' dinner.

Ryan tap-tap-tapped away at his laptop, piecing together the first chapter of the story. He used lots of creative tricks that he learned in Miss Butters' class,

'The alien's green skin dripped like bogies. He squelched and squeaked as he walked around the kitchen collecting plates. He threw some potatoes in

the blender and whizzed it together with grapefruit juice.

He peered into it and decided that it needed a little something extra. The alien pulled out some liquorice. "This will do just fine," he cackled.'

Ryan triple-checked his chapter for errors. He explored the blog page to find tools that would make his writing look more eye-catching.

"This is it. This is the first chapter of *Meals from Mars*." Ryan readied himself to click 'publish' on the blog page; the tiny button that was going to reveal his writing to the world; the launch for his mission.

Ryan nervously hovered the cursor over the button. Nobody had ever read his stories before. What if nobody liked it? What if they said it was terrible? What if people thought it was silly?

Ryan shook his head. To become a writer, he needed to show everyone how good he was. CLICK!

Chapter 7: The reviews!

"It sounds awesome. I'll read it as soon as I get home," said San. Ryan was persuading his friends to read the blog.

"I'm going shopping later, but I guess I can check it out after dinner." Sally agreed. She was very good at spreading rumours.

"Yeah, I'll read it, dude," agreed Tim. "It beats doing homework and chores." Tim was lazy but very popular; he would be good at spreading the word.

"Will you give me your honest opinion, Miss Butters?" asked Ryan.

Miss Butters sipped her endless supply of coffee. "Yes, of course. A true professional always gets feedback on their work!"

"Mr Adder tells me you are doing particularly well in maths," added Miss Butters. Thanks to the creepy kitten calendar, Ryan was keeping up with all his work.

That evening, Ryan endured another of Dad's alien dinners. Tonight's delight was strawberry laces in a raw onion and tomato sauce. Dad had placed a holly leaf on top as a garnish. Interesting.

Ryan reluctantly swallowed the last horrible bite of the gruesome meal before rushing to his room to see how many people had read the first chapter.

"Anything over ten, anything over ten," Ryan hoped. With his eyes hidden behind his fingers, he slowly peeked at the number of views.

"47! Yes!" That was good! Really good.

Ryan jumped up and down in his bedroom ecstatically.

"Ryan? What's 47? What's that graph on your screen?" Dad appeared in the doorway.

Ryan froze. Dad had discovered him! He shuffled in front of the screen. "Oh, it's maths homework. I, err, got the right answer to a difficult question. It was 47!"

Dad stared at Ryan suspiciously for what seemed like ages. “Ah, of course, well done” he said, finally. Phew! For the rest of the evening, Ryan contained his excitement. One day he would surprise Dad with an epic story to prove he was a great writer!

***

The following morning everyone trudged into assembly. The chatter in the school hall quietened as Mr Holiday timidly began speaking about litter and bad behavior. He droned, on and on and...

"And, er, as y-you may know, Ryan from 7B has started writing a blog."

Ryan jerked his head up in shock. Everyone muttered around him. How did Mr Holiday know about his blog?

"Quiet please!" Mr Holiday tried to sound authoritative but failed miserably. "Qu-quiet!" The murmuring gradually died down. "Yes, many of us have read it and, yes, it is an incredible opening to his story..." Ryan couldn't believe what he was hearing... "I think I speak f-for all of us when I say that we-we're looking forward to reading the next chapter t-t-tomorrow."

The hall erupted with cheers. They couldn't wait! Ryan didn't cheer. He was in shock. *Tomorrow?* He couldn't do another chapter by tomorrow! What was he going to do? He couldn't let everyone down.

The cheering grew louder as Ryan slowly stood up in the middle of the hall. He raised his hands to hush the crowd, "I'm sorry everyone," he announced, "the next chapter will be released next week."

The cheering stopped.

"But Holiday said it would be tomorrow," called out a voice from the back. Mr Holiday seemed concerned his assembly was being taken over by unruly students.

"We want to know what happens next. Does

the alien come to Earth?" Questions flew from around the room.

"I promise the next chapter will amaze and surprise you. You'll just have to wait a while longer," informed Ryan, taking his seat.

"Err, yes, s-settle down" continued Mr Holiday, "we'll, err, you'll just have to wait!"

And so the wait began...

Chapter 8: The next chapter

Ryan marched into maths, his head buzzing from the assembly. "Ryan, can I see you for a minute?" asked Mr Adder.

Oh no. His grades were slipping. Was Mr Adder about to set even more homework? He'd never get his next chapter done! They stepped to one side.

"I was wondering, Ryan, if you could tell me what happens to the alien chef?" he asked quietly, "You know, for your favourite teacher," he winked.

Ryan wasn't going to give up any secrets, especially to an imposter!

It turned out Ryan would be fending off teachers as well as students until he posted chapter two.

Even schoolkids Ryan had never met were asking about the story. "That was a great start to your blog! It's amazing!" said a random fair-haired student.

"Err thanks... er, you." said a flattered Ryan. Fame was proving to be time-consuming, keeping all these people happy!

"Jamie-May and Chardonnay can't wait any longer," complained Sally at lunchtime. A large group of Ryan's classmates crowded around him just as he was tucking into the salmon and custard roll Dad had prepared for him for lunch. "They just have to know when the next chapter will be out."

Ryan responded quickly. "Sorry everyone, it's not finished yet. You'll have to wait!"

San dropped his sandwich on the table and leapt to his feet. “Yeah, you heard the man. WAIT! Now step away and let him eat. Come on, move along, move along.”

The enthusiastic crowd finally broke away leaving Ryan in peace. “Thanks, San,” he whispered.

“No problem mate,” replied San. “But you’ll need to give them something to keep them going until next week. They’ll bother you even more, or worse - they’ll lose interest in the blog!”

Ryan chewed his lunch roll thoughtfully. San was right.

Ryan remembered something Miss Butters had said: “Writers often need to meet the demands of publishers or magazines. They have very tight deadlines!"

Ryan took a deep breath and clambered onto the dinner table. He towered over everyone in the canteen. Cheers erupted as heads turned to see him standing there.

"Good afternoon friends! I have with me the opening lines of chapter two!"

Cutlery clattered onto plates and conversations hushed. Ryan had everyone's attention.

"The ship fell through the sky like a missile. The alien peered through his windscreen and saw a vast green landscape through the clouds, filled with trees and farmland.

"Where am I?" he thought. An alarm buzzed loudly in the ship. If he didn't do something soon, he was going to crash onto this green planet."

Word spread like crazy over the next few days. Those lucky enough to have been in the canteen told all their friends about the beginning of the next chapter. They all told their families where to find the blog.

By now, an amazing 543 people had read Ryan's first chapter and were waiting for the next one! They would come banging at his front door, demanding to know what happens next. How would he explain that to Dad?

Chapter 9: Crash landing

Ryan stuck to his sickly kitten timetable and made sure he studied hard alongside his writing. He was striking the perfect balance and sure enough, by the end of the week, it was ready!

The alien salvaged what he could from the wreckage. He managed to pull out his sonic shaker and cosmic cooker and stashed them in his handbag.

"At least I can still cook my delicious treats!" he thought, setting off into

the night. Little did he know, he was being watched!

Once again, Ryan hovered his cursor over the 'publish' button. Everyone was expecting a great chapter; there was no going back. He was full of mixed emotions. Excited to see what everyone thought of his blog; nervous about his dad finding out.

He clicked to add the chapter to his blog.

Soon he would have a whole story on the Internet. He couldn't wait to show Dad what he had done. For now, though, it was a secret project. What if Dad found out?

***

The response to the second chapter was amazing! "It's brilliant Ryan," praised Miss Butters, "in fact, I would say it's better than the work you have done in my English lessons."

"Jamie-May and Chardonnay thought it was, like, the best." Sally had been busy gossiping about *Meals from Mars*. In fact, lots of people told Ryan about how much they liked the second chapter.

"I'm sorry if I rushed you before," apologised Mr Adder. "The second chapter was epic. That extra writing time really paid off." Ryan still wasn't sure if

Mr Adder was an imposter and hoped his stories weren't giving him sinister ideas.

What a day! Everyone loved his second chapter and Ryan was eager to begin the next one tonight. He breathed a huge sigh of relief as he arrived home from school.

Ryan slowly pushed open the front door and froze immediately. Stood right in the middle of the hallway was Dad, staring straight at Ryan.

"Err, Dad? Is everything okay? Why aren't you rustling up tonight's dinner? What's on the menu?" Ryan was a little taken aback by Dad's presence. Dad ignored Ryan's questions.

"I received an email today from my colleague at work," Dad said sternly, tapping his tablet computer. "Something about a new blog she had found about an *alien chef*. Written by someone going by the name of "Write-it Ryan."

Ryan's stomach dropped. The game was up. Dad had discovered his secret project! Ryan hadn't even finished writing the whole story. This was it. No more *Meals from Mars.*

Ryan panicked. What could he say? A thousand thoughts ran through his mind. There would be outrage. Everyone would be demanding the next chapter but it would never arrive. After such a promising beginning, the whole school would ridicule him, it would be awful.

Ryan didn't need a powerful computer to know what Dad was thinking, he was going to get a month's worth of chores!

After what felt like a year stood opposite Dad, Ryan began to mumble an explanation.

"I think I should explain. I'm sorry, Dad."

Dad continued staring at Ryan. He didn't utter a single word as he loaded the blog onto his tablet.

"I'm really sorry Dad. I made sure that I worked on my other subjects too. Miss Butters thought it would be a good way to see if I could handle being a writer when I grew up."

Still nothing.

"It was meant to be a secret. I was going to tell you when the book was finished." Ryan pleaded, sinking to the floor and putting his head between his hands.

"I really enjoyed reading your blog," smiled Dad.

"I know. I'm really sorry," said Ryan, "I'll go do chores for the rest of my life. I should never have disobeyed you."

"No, Ryan," Dad interrupted, "I'm trying to say I enjoyed..."

"I'll stop writing, Dad. I didn't mean to upset you..."

Ryan paused. "What? Dad? You enjoyed it?" Ryan was sure he'd misheard Dad.

"Yes, I did, as did my work friends. You really are a talented writer, Ryan," Dad chuckled heartily. "You found something you were good at and chose to share it with the world. I shouldn't have tried to stop you from writing."

"What, really?" Ryan was in disbelief. "Err, well, Thanks Dad."

"I called the school to ask about it. Mr Holiday told me that your grades are improving too. You've managed your time well, Ryan. Although, I must ask, was the alien chef based on me?" asked Dad, "he made some of the meals I make!"

Ryan thought fast. "Well, I was *inspired* by you, Dad. I always thought your cooking was like something from outer space!"

"Well, in that case, you'd better make sure that alien chef is the coolest alien in the universe!"

"He sure will be!" cheered Ryan.

"Great," said Dad. "Let's have dinner. How does sausage ice-cream pie with lemonade sauce sound?"

"Err, out of this world, Dad!" said Ryan. But he soon looked on the plus side - it gave him a great idea for the next chapter of *Meals from Mars*.

Chapter 3: The Poisoned Pie Plan!

THE END

Write-it Ryan is the fourth in the series of the Clever Tykes books. We really hoped you enjoyed reading it and we hope you'll check out the other titles in the series.

If you'd like to learn more about the Clever Tykes books visit www.CleverTykes.com. We'd love to hear from you!

You'll find us on Facebook (/CleverTykes) and follow Clever Tykes on Twitter @CleverTykes

Written by Ben, Jodie and Jason.

Printed in Great Britain
by Amazon

43288609R00051